Covered Bridges of the North
by
Harold Stiver

Copyright Statement
Covered Bridges of the North
A Guide for Photographers and Explorers

Copyright 2024 Harold Stiver

License Notes
All rights reserved. No part of this book may be reproduced in any form or by any electronic or mechanical means including information storage and retrieval systems without permission in writing from the author, except by the reviewer who may quote brief passages.
Version 1.0

ISBN #978-1-927835-46-3

Table of Contents

How to use this Book	7
Photographing Covered Bridges	10
A Short History of Covered Bridges	12

Illinois Bridges
Illinois County Map	14

Boone County
Rockford Bolt Co. (Young)	15

Bureau County
Red	16
Captain Swift	17

Cumberland County
Jackson	18

Henderson County
Allaman, Eames, Henderson County	19

Kendall County
Stickleback	20

Knox County
Wolf	21

Randolph County
Little Mary's River	22

Sangamon County
Glenarm (Hedley, Sugar Creek)	23

Shelby County
Thompson Mill	24

Illinois Bridge Tour
Illinois North Tour	25
Illinois South Tour	26

Iowa Bridges
Iowa County Map	27

Madison County
Cutler (Donahoe) 28
Hogback 29

Holliwell 30
Imes (King, Munger, Mills) 31
Roseman (Oak Grove) 32
Cedar 33
Marion County
Hammond 34
Wilcox Game Preserve 35
Knoxville 36
Polk County
Owens 37
Iowa Bridge Tours
Madison County Tour 38
Marion and Polk Counties Tour 39

Michigan Bridges
Michigan County Map 40
Ionia County
White's 41
Kent County
Ada (Bradfield) 42
Fallasburg 43
Saginaw County
Zehnder (Holtz Brucke) 44
St. Joseph County
Langley 45
Wayne County
Ackley 46
Michigan Bridge Tour 47

Minnesota Bridge
Minnesota County Map 48

Goodhue County
Zumbrota   49

South Dakota Bridge
South Dakota County Map   50
Edgemount City Park   51

Wisconsin Bridges
Wisconsin County Map   52
Grant County
Stonefield Village   53
Ozaukee County
Cedarburg   54
Price County
Smith Rapids (Chequamegon)   55
Waupaca County
Red Mill   56
Waushara County
Springwater Volunteer   57
Wisconsin Bridge Tour   58

Glossary   59
Truss Types   61
Recently Lost   68
References   69
Photo Credits   70
The Photographer's and Explorer's Series   71

Illinois Index   73
Iowa Index   73
Michigan Index   74
Minnesota Index   74
South Dakota Index   74
Wisconsin Index   74

How to use this Book

For each of the 33 historical or Traditional Covered Bridges remaining in Illinois, Iowa, Michigan, Minnesota, South Dakota and Wisconsin we have included photographs as well as descriptive and statistical data. Traditional Covered Bridges are those that follow the building practices of the Nineteenth Century and the early part of the Twentieth Century or those built later that follow those methods. All of these bridges have had repairs done as portions wear out, and some may have been almost entirely replaced through the years. I have used "The National Society for the Preservation of Covered Bridges, Inc." list of what they consider as Traditional Bridges.

Following is data included for each bridge

Name: This is listed in bold type, and where there are other names, it is the common name or the name listed on an accompanying plaque.

Other Names: Beside the Common Name in brackets, you will find other names that the bridge has been known by.

Nearest County and Township are listed.

It is frustrating to go on an excursion to see something and not be able to find it. This book offers you multiple ways to ensure that doesn't happen.

GPS Position: This is our recommended method. Enter the coordinates in a good GPS unit and it should take you right there. You, of course, must use care that you are not led off road or on a dangerous route.

Detailed Driving Directions: Directions from a town near to the bridge.

Builder: If known, the name of the original builder(s) is listed.

Year Built: As well as the year built, if it has been moved it will shown with the year preceded by the letter M and, if a major repair has been done, the year will be shown preceded by the letter R.

Truss Type: The type for the particular bridge will be listed. If you are interested in more information on the various types of trusses, access "Truss Types" from the Table of Contents.

Dimensions: The length and number of spans

Notes: A place where you can find additional items of interest about the bridge.

World Index Number:
Covered bridges are assigned a number to keep track of them which consists of three numbers separated by hyphens.

The first number represents the number of the U.S. State in alphabetical order. Following number 50 for the 50th state are additional numbers for Canadian provinces. Thus the numbers 05 represents California.

The second set of numbers represents the county of that state, again based on alphabetical order. Humboldt is the 12th county alphabetically in California, and it is designated as 05-12.

Each bridge in that county is given a number as it was discovered or built. Zane's Ranch was the fifth bridge discovered or built in the County of Humboldt, California and it therefore has the designation of 05-12-05. Sometimes you will see the first set of numbers replaced by the abbreviation for the state, thus CA-12-05.

A bridge is sometimes substantially rebuilt or replaced and it then has the suffix #2 added to it.

National Register of Historic Places: If the bridge has registered, the date is given.

Photographing Covered Bridges

Some standard positions
Portal: Taken to show the ends of bridge or bridge opening. This view, usually symmetrical, will include various signs posted. This is also a good way to get run over, so be careful!
3/4 view: Shows both the front and sides of the bridge, and is often the most attractive.
Side view: Taken from a bank or from the river, this gives not only a nice view of the bridge but usually allows for some interesting foreground elements.
Interior view: An image taken from the interior of the bridge will show some interesting structure but there is not a lot of available light. A tripod is important and HDR processing is helpful.
Landscape View: With the bridge smaller in the frame, you can introduce the habitat around it, particularly effective with colorful autumn foliage.

Using HDR(High Dynamic Range)
HDR is a process where multiple images of varying exposure are combined to make one image.

It has a bad name with some people because many HDR images are super-saturated, a kind of digital age version of an Elvis painted on velvet. However, the process is actually about getting a full range of exposure with no burnt out highlights or blocked shadows. This is an ideal processing solution for photographing Covered Bridges where you often have open light sky set against dark shadowed landscape and structure.

I use a series of three exposures at levels of -1 2/3, 0, +1 2/3, and this normally runs the full exposure range encountered. It is important to use a stable tripod.

One situation where you may need a larger series is shooting from within a bridge and using the window to frame an outside scene. The dynamic range is huge and you will need to have a series with a much larger range.

There are a number of software programs you can use to combine these images including newer editions of Photoshop. I use Photomatix which I have found very versatile and easy to use.

Best times for photographing bridges
Mornings and evenings are generally the best times for outdoor photography but the use of HDR processing makes it easier even in bright direct light. Although any season is good for bridge photography including the winter, fall foliage included in a scene can be spectacular.

A Short History of Covered Bridges

Let's deal with that often posed question; "Why were the bridges covered"

1. Crossing animals thought it was a barn and entered easily. I like this suggestion, it shows imagination. However, its not the answer although the original bridges normally had no windows and this is said to be because animals would not be spooked by the sight of the water.

2. To cover up the unsightly truss structure. I don't think those early pioneers were that sensitive, and personally, I like the look of the trusses.

3. To keep snow off the travelled portion. In fact the bridge owners often paid to have the insides "snowed" in order to facilitate sleighs.

4. It offered some privacy to courting couples, hence "kissing bridges". That is a nice romantic notion but no.

In fact, the bridge was covered for economic reasons. The truss system was where much of the bridge's cost was found, and if left open to the elements, it deteriorated and the bridge became unstable and unsafe. Covering it protected this valuable portion and the roof could be replaced as needed with inexpensive materials and unskilled labour. Without coverings, a bridge might only have a life span of a decade while one that was covered often lasted 75 years or more before repairs became necessary. Besides extending the longevity of a bridge, wooden covered bridges had the virtue that they could be constructed of local materials and there were many available workers skilled in working with wood.

The first known Covered Bridge in North America was built in 1804 by Theodore Burr. It was called the Waterford bridge and it spanned the Hudson River in New York.

For the rest of the century and into the 20th Century, Covered bridge building boomed as the country became populated and people needed to travel between communities. The cost of constructing and maintaining a bridge was normally borne by the nearby community and many bridges charged a toll as a method of offsetting these costs.

The period from 1825 to 1875 was the heyday of bridge building but near the end of that period iron bridges began to supplant them.

The number of Covered bridges may have numbered 10,000 but have now dropped to about 840 spread throughout North America. Many have Historical Designations which provides them protection and many communities are interested in protecting their local historical bridges.

Illinois County Map

Rockford Bolt Co. (Young) CB
County: Boone, Illinois
Township: North Caledonia

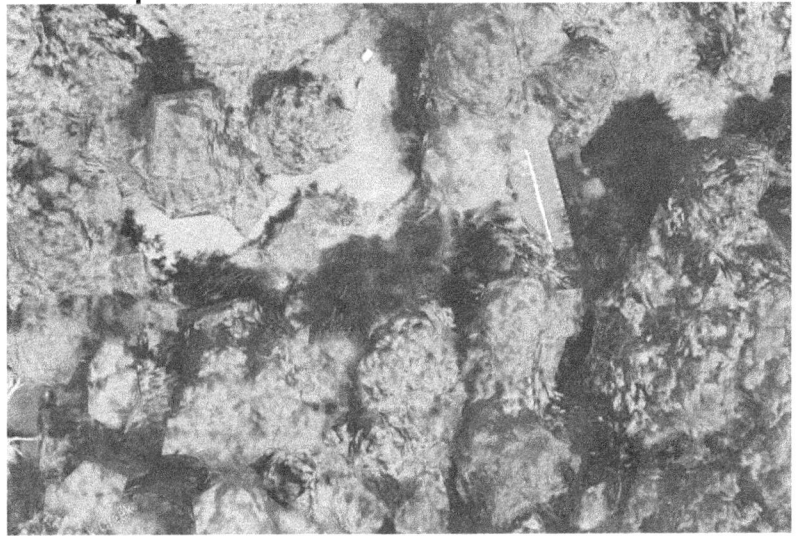

GPS Position: 42°24'41.0"N 88°56'22.0"W
Directions: From Roscoe, head east on Chestnut St for 250 ft and continue onto Burr Oak Rd. After 2.6 mi turn left onto Lovesee Rd where the bridge is 0.5 mi
Crosses: Kinnikinnick Creek
Carries: Lovesee Rd
Builder: Not known
Year Built: 1890 (M1968)
Truss Type: Howe
Dimensions: 1 Span, 75 feet
Notes: The bridge was built in 1890 to take finished product from their plant. They decided to demolish it in 1968 but agreed that a Mr. Walquist could have it if he removed it. This bridge is on private property

World Index Number: IL/13-04-01
National Register of Historic Places: Not listed

Red Covered Bridge
County: Bureau, Illinois
Township: Dover

GPS Position: 41°24'59.0"N 89°28'43.0"W
Directions: From Princeton, head north on IL-26 N from I-80 for 0.6 mi and turn left onto County Rd 1990 E. After 0.2 mi continue onto County Rd 1950 E and the bridge is 0.4 mi
Crosses: Big Bureau Creek
Carries: County Rd 1950 E
Builder: Not known
Year Built: 1863
Truss Type: Howe
Dimensions: 1 Span, 93 feet

Notes: This structure has recently been damaged by trucks in 2021 and 2023. It is currently closed to vehicle traffic after the second incident

World Index Number: IL/13-06-01
National Register of Historic Places: Listed April 23, 1975

Captain Swift Covered Bridge
County: Bureau, Illinois
Township: Princeton

GPS Position: 41°22'44.0"N 89°29'52.0"W
Directions: From Princeton, head west on Co Rd 1650 N/W Railroad Ave for 1.5 mi and turn left onto N Epperson Rd. After 0.3 mi turn right onto 1600 N Ave where the site is 0.3 mi
Crosses: Big Bureau Creek
Carries: 1600 N Ave
Builder: Willett Hofmann & Associates, Inc.
Year Built: 2007
Truss Type: Pratt variant and Arches
Dimensions: 1 Span, 128 feet

Notes: Swift Covered Bridge is the only two-lane covered bridge in Illinois. It is in a very picturesque setting just west of Princeton.

World Index Number: IL/13-06-05
National Register of Historic Places: Not listed

Jackson Covered Bridge
County: Cumberland, Illinois
Township: Greenup

GPS Position: 39°14'20.0"N 88°11'14.0"W
Directions: From Greenup, head southwest on W Cumberland St for 1.9 mi to see the bridge
Crosses: Embarras River
Carries: W Cumberland St

Builder: Rhutasel and Associates, Inc.
Year Built: 2000
Truss Type: Multiple King with Arches
Dimensions: 1 Span, 191.5 feet

Notes: This bridge is a replica of the National Road Bridge that was constructed at this location in 1832 and destroyed in 1865.

World Index Number: IL/13-18-01#2
National Register of Historic Places: Not listed

Allaman (Eames, Henderson County) CB
County: Henderson, Illinois
Township: Gladstone

GPS Position: 40°53'39.0"N 90°56'57.0"W
Directions: From Gladstone, head north on State Hwy 164 N for 1.9 mi and turn right, into Henderson County Covered Bridge Park and the bridge
Crosses: Henderson Creek
Carries: Pedestrian walkway

Builder: Jacob Allaman
Year Built: 1865
Truss Type: Burr Arch
Dimensions: 1 Span, 104 feet
Notes: The bridge was closed to traffic in 1936 and became a pedestrian walkway and a picnic area was opened. The bridge was added to the National Register of Historic Places in 1975.

World Index Number: IL/13-36-01#2
National Register of Historic Places: February 24, 1975

Stickleback Covered Bridge
County: Kendall, Illinois
Township: Newark

GPS Position: 41°35'09.0"N 88°35'20.0"W
Directions: From Millbrook, head west on Whitfield Rd for 0.4 mi and turn left onto Rogers Rd. After 0.3 mi turn left on Finnie Rd and in 2.2 mi turn left on an unnamed road and the bridge
Crosses: stream
Carries: Unnamed road

Builder: William W. Davis
Year Built: 2000
Truss Type: Town
Dimensions: 1 Span, 45 feet

Notes: The bridge is on private property. It was built by Mr. Davis and friends from reclaimed materials.

World Index Number: IL/13-47-02
National Register of Historic Places: Not listed

Wolf Covered Bridge
County: Knox, Illinois
Township: Haw Creek

GPS Position: 40°51'24.0"N 90°06'36.0"W
Directions: From Knoxville, head east on Knox Hwy 17 for 7.7 mi and turn left to stay on Knox Hwy 17. Drive 0.6 mi to the bridge
Crosses: Spoon River
Carries: Knox Hwy 17
Builder: Not known
Year Built: 2020
Truss Type: Howe
Dimensions: 1 Span, 102 feet

Notes: The original 1865 covered bridge was destroyed in an arson attack in 1994. This replacement was built in the traditional manner and opened in 1999

World Index Number: IL/13-48-01#2
National Register of Historic Places: Not listed

Little Mary's River Covered Bridge
County: Randolph, Illinois
Township: Chester

GPS Position: 37°56'55.0"N 89°45'57.0"W
Directions: From Chester, head northeast on State Rte 150 E/State St for 4.3 mi and you will see the bridge
Crosses: Little Mary's River
Carries: State Rte 150

Builder: Plank Road Company
Year Built: 1854 (R2005)
Truss Type: Burr Arch
Dimensions: 1 Span, 98 feet

Notes: Built in 1854, it is the oldest surviving covered bridge in Illinois. It was closed to vehicle traffic in 1930. It was restored in 2005

World Index Number: IL/13-79-01
National Register of Historic Places: December 31, 1974

Glenarm (Hedley, Sugar Creek) CB
County: Sangamon, Illinois
Township: Ball

GPS Position: 39°38'25.0"N 89°39'43.0"W
Directions: From Chatham, head east on E Walnut St for 0.8 mi and turn right onto Gordon Dr. After 1.2 mi turn left to stay on Gordon Dr and drive 1.5 mi. Turn left onto Covered Bridge Rd and the bridge is 1.3 mi
Crosses: Sugar Creek
Carries: Covered Bridge Rd
Builder: Thomas Black
Year Built: c1880 (R1965)
Truss Type: Multiple King variant and Burr Arch
Dimensions: 1 Span, 58 feet
Notes: In 1965, repairs to the bridge included repairs to side boards and a new roof as well as work on the abutments. It was closed to vehicles in 1984 and a picnic area was built around it.
World Index Number: IL/13-84-02
National Register of Historic Places: January 9, 1978

Thompson Mill Covered Bridge
County: Shelby, Illinois
Township: Dry Point

GPS Position: 39°15'30.0"N 88°49'05.0"W
Directions: From Crowden, head east on Co Hwy 11/E Locust St for 2.0 mi and turn left onto N 1725 E Rd. After 1.0 mi turn left onto 1790 E/E 300 N Rd and find the bridge
Crosses: Kaskaskia River
Carries: 1790 E/E 300 N Rd
Builder: Not known
Year Built: 1868
Truss Type: Howe
Dimensions: 1 Span, 105 feet
Notes: This bridge was built in Michigan and shipped to its current site. It is closed to vehicle traffic. It is named for the nearby mill which was in business until 1914.

World Index Number: IL/13-87-01
National Register of Historic Places: March 13, 1975

Illinois North Tour

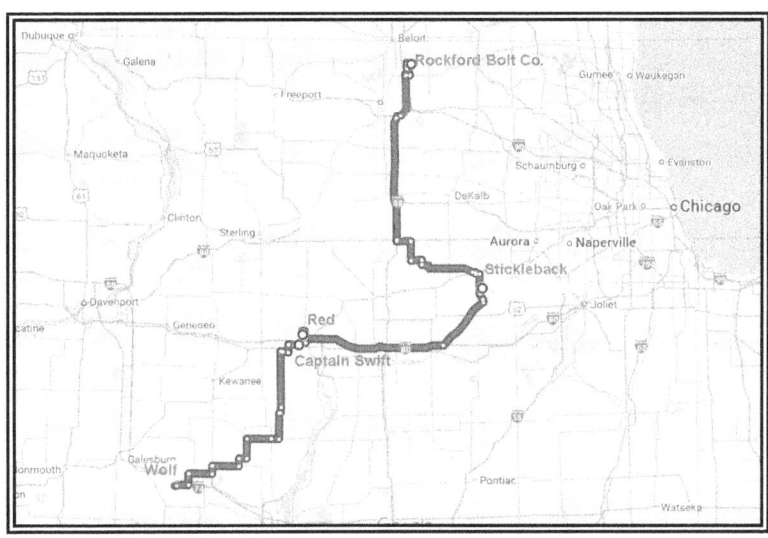

5 Bridges, 4 hours driving

Rockford Bolt Co.	42°24'41.0"N 88°56'22.0"W
Stickleback	41°35'09.0"N 88°35'20.0"W
Red	41°24'59.0"N 89°28'43.0"W
Captain Swift	41°22'44.0"N 89°29'52.0"W
Wolf	40°51'24.0"N 90°06'36.0"W

The last bridge on this tour (Wolf) is an 1 hour drive from the first bridge (Allaman) in Tour2

Illinois South Tour

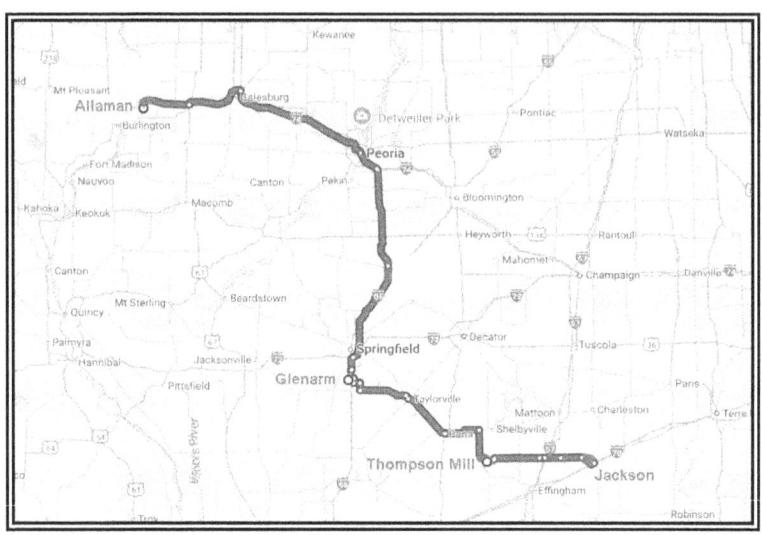

4 Bridges, 5 hours driving

Allaman	40°53'39.0"N 90°56'57.0"W
Glenarm	39°38'25.0"N 89°39'43.0"W
Thompson Mill	39°15'30.0"N 88°49'05.0"W
Jackson	39°14'20.0"N 88°11'14.0"W

The only bridge not included in the tours is Little Mary's River Covered Bridg, an outlier near the southern border. It is 2.5 hours driving from the last bridge on this tour (Jackson)

Iowa County Map

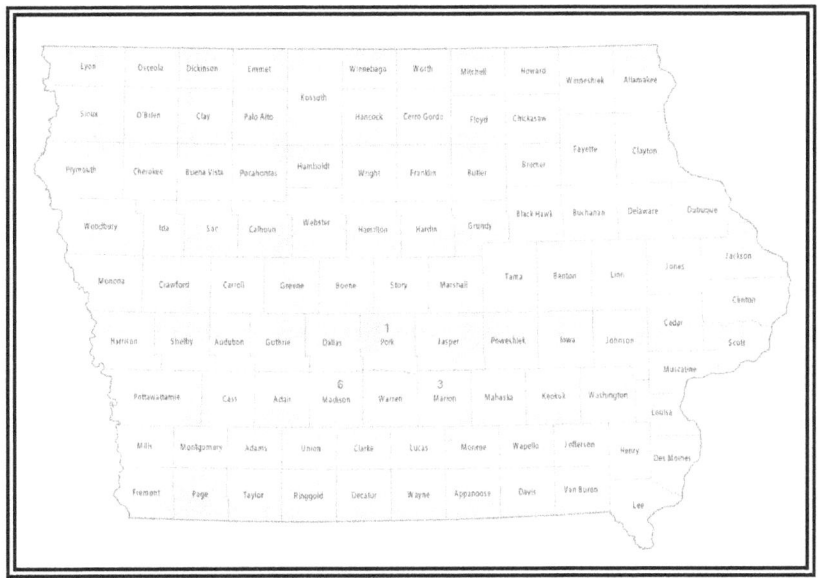

Cutler (Donahoe) Covered Bridge
County: Madison, Iowa
Township: Douglas

GPS Position: 41°19'52.0"N 94°00'18.7"W
Directions: From Winterset, head east on E High St toward S 2nd St from John Wayne Drive for 0.4 mi and the bridge is on the right
Crosses: Brook
Carries: Pedestrian walkway
Builder: Eli Cox and his sons George, John, and Alfred
Year Built: !871 (M1979) (R1997)
Truss Type: Town
Dimensions: 1 Span, 79 feet
Notes: This bridge was originally near Bevington over the North River but was moved to Winterset's City Park in 1979. It is closed to vehicle traffic. Cutler and Donahoe were families who lived nearby

World Index Number: IA/15-61-02
National Register of Historic Places: October 8, 1976

Hogback Covered Bridge
County: Madison, Iowa
Township: Douglas

GPS Position: 41°23'11.9"N 94°02'54.2"W
Directions: From Winterset, head north on Hogback Bridge Rd for 1.6 miles where you will find the bridge
Crosses: North River
Carries: Hogback Bridge Rd

Builder: Harvey P. Jones and George K. Foster
Year Built: 1884
Truss Type: Town
Dimensions: 1 Span, 106 feet

Notes: Like most of the Madison County Covered Bridges, it has a flat roof. It received a substantial rehabilitation in 1992 and continues to carry vehicle traffic.

World Index Number: IA/15-61-04
National Register of Historic Places: August 28, 1976

Holliwell Covered Bridge
County: Madison, Iowa
Township: Scott

GPS Position: 41°19'21.0"N 93°57'33.0"W
Directions: From Winterset, head east on E Court Ave for 1.4 mi and turn right onto Norwood Ave. After 0.3 mi make a left onto Holliwell Bridge Rd. In 1.8 mi turn right, the site is 0.1 mi
Crosses: Middle River
Carries: Holliwell Bridge Rd
Builder: Harvey P. Jones and George K. Foster
Year Built: 1880 (R1995)
Truss Type: Double arch and town
Dimensions: 1 Span, 113 feet

Notes: This is the longest surviving covered bridge in Iowa. It underwent an extensive renovation in 1995. It is closed to vehicle traffic

World Index Number: IA/15-61-05
National Register of Historic Places: August 28, 1976

Imes (King, Munger, Mills) Covered Bridge
County: Madison, Iowa
Township: South

GPS Position: 41°17'18.0"N 93°47'56.0"W
Directions: From St Charles, head east on W Main St for 0.4 mi and turn right onto Imes Bridge Rd and the bridge is 0.1 mi
Crosses: brook
Carries: Imes Bridge Rd
Builder: Not known
Year Built: 1870 (M1887) (M1977) (R1977)
Truss Type: Town
Dimensions: 1 Span, 81 feet

Notes: This is the oldest surviving covered bridge in Iowa and a bit of a traveller. It was moved in 1877 from over the North River to Clanton Creek. It was moved again to its present site in 1977. It is closed to vehicle traffic

World Index Number: IA/15-61-06
National Register of Historic Places: February 9, 1979

Roseman (Oak Grove) Covered Bridge
County: Madison, Iowa
Township: Jackson

GPS Position: 41°17'31.0"N 94°09'05.0"W
Directions: From Macksburg, head north on East St for 0.4 mi then go on Co Rd P53 for 4.4 mi. Turn right onto Carriage Trail and in 1.7 mi turn left onto Elder Berry Ave. After 0.6 mi, continue onto Co Rd G47 for 0.2 mi and the bridge
Crosses: Middle River
Carries: Co Rd G47

Builder: Harvey P. Jones and George K. Foster
Year Built: 1883 (R1992)
Truss Type: Town and Queen
Dimensions: 1 Span, 107 feet
Notes: The bridge is closed to vehicle traffic. It is frequently referenced in The Bridges of Madison County. It was rehabilitated in 1992.

World Index Number: IA/15-61-07
National Register of Historic Places: September 1, 1976

Cedar Covered Bridge
County: Madison, Iowa
Township: Union

GPS Position: 41°21'54.0"N 93°59'25.0"W
Directions: From Winterset, head north on Cedar Bridge Rd for 1.5 mi and continue onto Lakeside Ln. In 0.1 mi, continue onto Cedar Bridge Rd/Cedar Bridge Trail and the site
Crosses: Cedar Creek
Carries: Cedar Bridge Trail
Builder: Not known
Year Built: 2019
Truss Type: Town and Queen
Dimensions: 1 Span, 76 feet
Notes: This is the 3rd bridge here. The first was built in 1883 and lost to arson in 2002. The second, built in 2004, was lost to arson in 2017. The present structure opened in 2019 and is Iowa's youngest

World Index Number: IA/15-61-B
National Register of Historic Places: Not listed

Hammond Covered Bridge
County: Marion, Iowa
Township: Indiana

GPS Position: 41°10'39.0"N 93°00'50.0"W
Directions: From the town of Indiana, head south on 170th Pl for 2.0 mi and turn right to stay on 170th Pl and see the bridge
Crosses: North Cedar Creek
Carries: 170th Pl

Builder: S.F. Collins
Year Built: 1894 (R2004)
Truss Type: Howe
Dimensions: 1 Span, 80 feet

Notes: This bridge was proposed by Samuel Hammond who lived nearby. It was approved and opened in 1894 and was named for him. The deck is laid upon steel stringers.

World Index Number: IA/15-63-01
National Register of Historic Places: May 15, 1998

Wilcox Game Preserve Covered Bridge
County: Marion, Iowa
Township: Liberty

GPS Position: 41°14'09.0"N 92°57'06.0"W
Directions: From Attica, head east on IA-5 S for 1.4 mi and turn left onto Marion County Hwy T17. After 1.5 mi, turn right and the bridge is a short way
Crosses: North Cedar Creek
Carries: Game Preserve Road
Builder: Not known
Year Built: 1870 (M1970)
Truss Type: Town
Dimensions: 1 Span, 40 feet

Notes: This bridge and the Knoxville Covered Bridge were part of the Marysville Covered Bridge which was split in half and moved to their respective sites in 1970

World Index Number: IA/15-63-04
National Register of Historic Places: Not listed

Knoxville Covered Bridge
County: Marion, Iowa
Township: Knoxville

GPS Position: 41°18'59.0"N 93°07'33.0"W
Directions: From Knoxville, head west on W Pleasant St for 0.6 mi and turn left onto Willetts Dr. After 0.3 mi turn right into Marion County Park and the bridge is 0.4 mi
Crosses: ravine
Carries: Marion County Park road
Builder: Not known
Year Built: 1870 (M1970)
Truss Type: Town
Dimensions: 1 Span, 41 feet
Notes: This bridge and the Wilcox Game Preserve Covered Bridge were part of the Marysville Covered Bridge which was split in half and moved to their respective sites in 1970
World Index Number: IA/15-63-05
National Register of Historic Places: Not listed

Owens Covered Bridge
County: Polk, Iowa
Township: Bloomfield

GPS Position: 41°32'25.0"N 93°33'35.0"W
Directions: From Des Moines, head southeast on Indianola Ave for 0.6 mi and turn left onto Easter Lake Dr. After 0.8 mi turn left onto Easter Lake Park and the bridge is 0.2 mi
Crosses: arm of the Yeader Creek
Carries: Walkway
Builder: Sam Gray
Year Built: 1887 or 1888 (M1968)
Truss Type: Howe
Dimensions: 1 Span, 100 feet

Notes: This bridge was originally located over the North River. It was moved a few miles to the present location in 1968. It is closed to vehicle traffic

World Index Number: IA/15-77-01
National Register of Historic Places: Not listed

Iowa Bridge Tours
The following tours are an efficient order to visit multiple sites

Madison County Tour

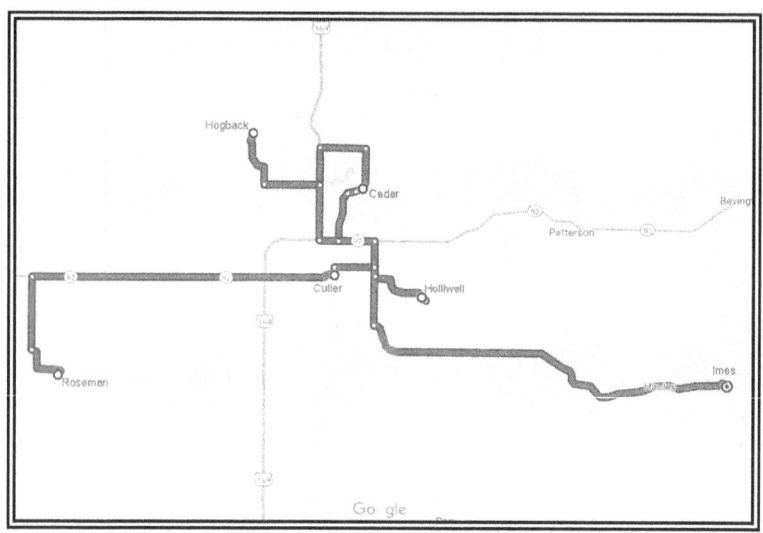

6 Bridges, 1 hour 15 minutes driving

Roseman (Oak Grove)	41°17'31.0"N 94°09'05.0"W
Cutler (Donahoe)	41°19'52.0"N 94°00'18.7"W
Holliwell	41°19'21.0"N 93°57'33.0"W
Cedar	41°21'54.0"N 93°59'25.0"W
Hogback	41°23'11.9"N 94°02'54.2"W
Imes (King, Munger, Mills)	41°17'18.0"N 93°47'56.0"W

If you wish to visit all of the Iowa bridges, the last Madison County Bridge (Imes) is 30 minutes drive from the first Marion and Polk Counties Bridge (Owens)

Marion and Polk Counties Tour

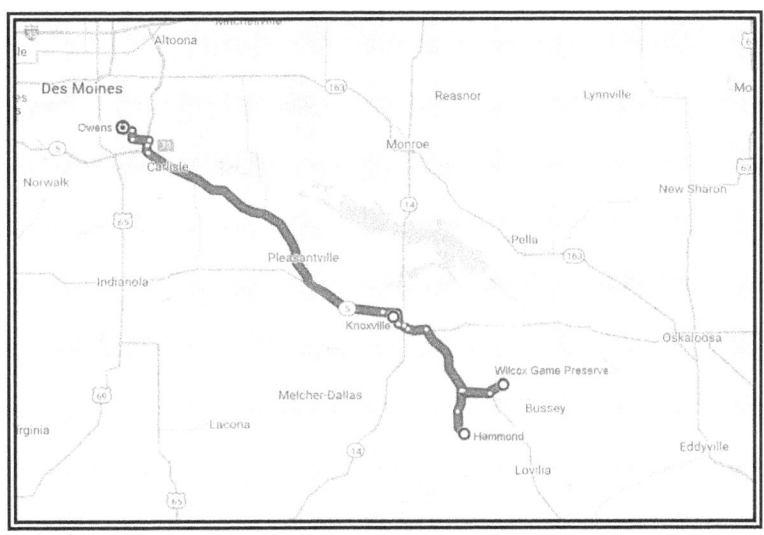

4 Bridges, 1 hour 15 minutes driving

Owens	41°32'25.0"N 93°33'35.0"W
Knoxville	41°18'59.0"N 93°07'33.0"W
Wilcox Game Preserve	41°14'09.0"N 92°57'06.0"W
Hammond	41°10'39.0"N 93°00'50.0"W

If you wish to visit all of the Iowa bridges, the last Madison County Bridge (Imes) is 30 minutes drive from the first Marion and Polk Counties Bridge (Owens)

Michigan County Map

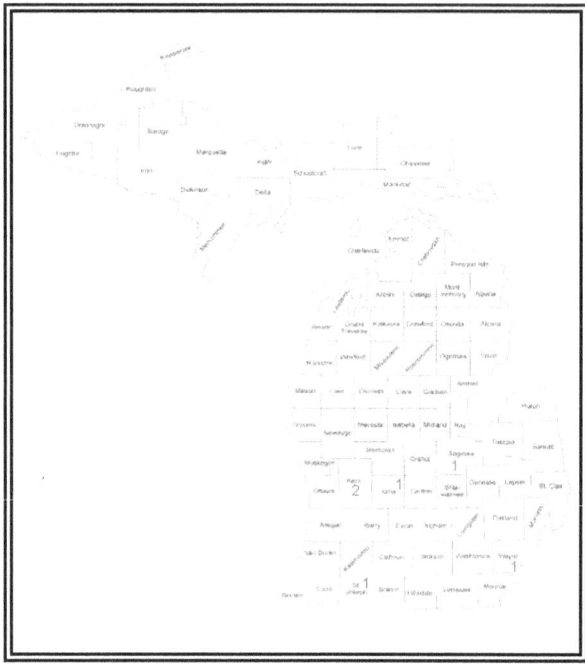

White's Covered Bridge
County: Ionia, Michigan
Township: Keene

GPS Position: N 43° 00.902' W 85° 17.864'
Directions: In Smyrna, head SW on Whites Bridge Rd for 1.3 mi and left to stay on Whites Bridge Rd, the bridge is 2.6 mi
Crosses: Flat River
Carries: Whites Bridge Rd,
Builder: AECOM
Year Built: 2020
Truss Type: Brown
Dimensions: 1 Span, 116 feet
Notes: The original 1869 covered bridge at this site was destroyed in an arson attack in 2013. By 2015, the Whites Bridge Historical Society announced that funding had been obtained to replace the structure. A replica was completed in 2020, although it was strengthened so that the load limit could be raised.
World Index Number: MI/22-34-01#2
National Register of Historic Places: Not listed

Ada (Bradfield) Covered Bridge
County: Kent, Michigan
Township: Ada

GPS Position: N 42° 57.137' W 85° 29.153'
Directions: From Ada, take Ada Dr. south off of MI-21 and turn left on Thorneapple River Dr. And the bridge is a short distance at a town park.
Crosses: Thorneapple River
Carries: Thorneapple River Dr
Builder: Town of Ada
Year Built: 1980 (Original 1867)
Truss Type: Howe
Dimensions: 1 Span, 125 feet
Notes: This bridge replaced an 1867 one that was destroyed by fire in 1979. The original was built on the Brown Truss system which was only used in Michigan.

World Index Number: MI/22-41-01#2
National Register of Historic Places: Not listed

Fallasburg Covered Bridge
County: Kent, Michigan
Township: Vergennes

GPS Position: N 42° 58.845' W 85° 19.663'
Directions: From Lowell take Hudson Rd north from MI-21 for 3.2 miles and go right on Fallasburg Park Dr. for 0.7 miles to Covered Bridge Rd. where you will see the bridge
Crosses: Flat River
Carries: Covered Bridge Road
Builder: Jared N. Bresee
Year Built: 1862 or 1871 (R1905) (1945) (R1994)
Truss Type: Brown
Dimensions: 1 Span, 100 feet
Notes: This bridge was constructed using the Brown Truss which was only used for 4 Michigan Bridges, three of which survive. It is described as similar to the Howe Truss of "X" bracing.

World Index Number: MI/22-41-02
National Register of Historic Places: March 16, 1972

Zehnder (Holtz Brucke) Covered Bridge
County: Saginaw, Michigan
Township: Frankenmuth

GPS Position: N 43° 19.535' W 83° 44.334'
Directions: From the center of Frankenmuth turn east off MI-83/Main St. and you will see the bridge
Crosses: Cass River
Carries: Covered Bridge Lane
Builder: Graton and Associates
Year Built: 1980
Truss Type: Town
Dimensions: 3 Spans, 239 feet
Notes: This is quite an impressive bridge with two lanes for traffic and two for pedestrians. Although built in 1980, it was done in an authentic manner. Graton and Associates completed the 230 ton structure on the river bank and then, with a series of block, capstan, comealongs and pulleys, pulled it into place using only two oxen
World Index Number: MI/22-73-02
National Register of Historic Places: Not listed

Langley Covered Bridge
County: St. Joseph, Michigan
Township: Lockport

GPS Position: N 41° 58.075' W 85° 31.706'
Directions: From Centerville, go north on Covered Bridge Road/ County Rd 133 for 3.0 miles to reach the bridge site
Crosses: St. Joseph River
Carries: Covered Bridge Road
Builder: Pierce Bodner
Year Built: 1887 (R1951) (2023)
Truss Type: Howe
Dimensions: 3 Span, 282 Feet
Notes: Langley is one of the longest covered bridges surviving in North America. One of the striking things about this structure is how low it is to the water. In fact, it was raised 8 feet in 1910 when the Sturgis dam was built. In 2023, $3,200,000 was allotted for repairs

World Index Number: MI/22-75-01
National Register of Historic Places: Not listed

Ackley (Greenfield) Covered Bridge
County: Wayne, Michigan
Township: Dearborn

GPS Position: N 42° 18.256' W 83° 13.399'
Directions: From Michigan Ave, west of L-94 in Dearborn, take Oakland Blvd to Greenfield Village
Crosses: Pond
Carries: None
Builder: Joshua Ackley & Daniel Clouse
Year Built: 1832 (M1937)
Truss Type: Multiple King
Dimensions: 1 Span, 75 Feet
Notes: This early bridge was given to Henry Ford by the builder's granddaughter and moved from Pennsylvania in 1937 to Greenfield Village, Ford's exhibit of homes and workplaces. Note that the exhibit is only open in certain seasons and hours and their is an admission.

World Index Number: MI/22-82-01 (Formerly PA/38-30-41)
National Register of Historic Places: Not Listed

Michigan Bridge Tour

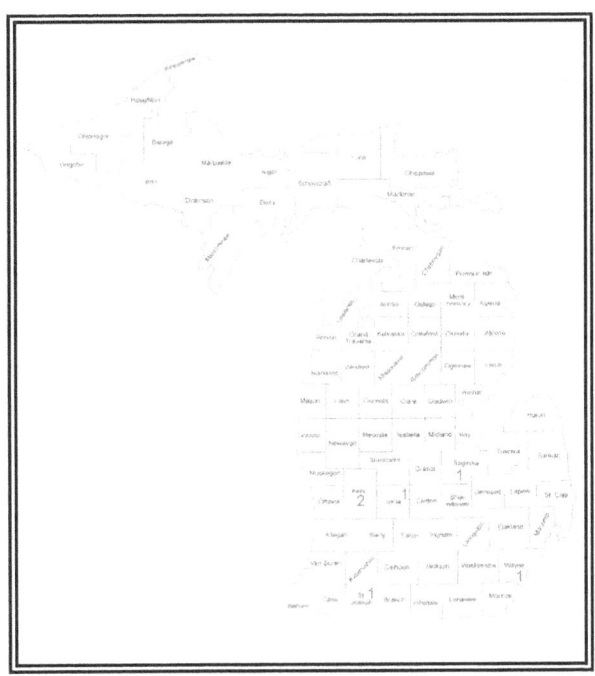

6 Bridges, 5 hours 30 minutes driving

Ackley	N 42° 18.256' W 83° 13.399'
Zehnder	N 43° 19.535' W 83° 44.334'
White's	N 43° 00.902' W 85° 17.864'
Fallasburg	N 42° 58.845' W 85° 19.663'
Ada	N 42° 57.137' W 85° 29.153'
Langley	N 41° 58.075' W 85° 31.706'

Minnesota County Map

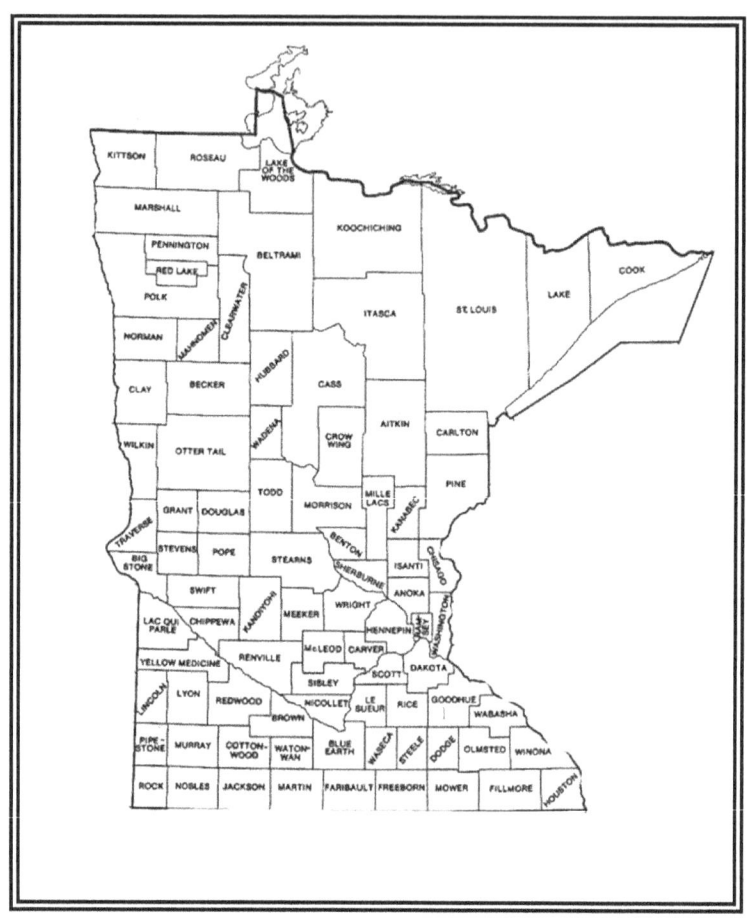

Zumbroto Covered Bridge
County: Goodhue, Minnesota
Township: Zumbroto

GPS Position: 44°17'46.8"N 92°40'13.6"W
Crosses: Zumbrota River
Carries: West Ave
Directions: In the town of Zumbrota, head north on Hiawatha Pioneer Trl/S Main St from E 3rd St and turn left at the 1st cross street onto W 2nd St. After 322 ft, turn right onto West Ave and find the bridge
Builder: Evander L. Kingsbury
Year Built: 1869 (M1932) (M1970) (R1970) (M1997) (R2019)
Truss Type: Lattice variant
Dimensions: 2 Spans, 116 feet
Notes: While the bridge was opened in 1869, it was not covered until 1871. It has been moved twice, finally resting at Zumbrota Covered Bridge Park. It is closed to vehicle traffic.

World Index Number: MN/23-25-01
National Register of Historic Places: February 20, 1975

South Dakota County Map

Edgemont City Park Covered Bridge
County: Fall River, South Dakota
Township: Edgemont

GPS Position: 43°17'54.1"N 103°49'26.9"W
Directions: 1948 2nd Ave, Edgemont
Crosses: pond
Carries: Pedestrian walkway
Builder: Moses Borntreger
Year Built: 2011
Truss Type: Town
Dimensions: 1 Span, 120 feet
Notes: This bridge is said to be the 3rd one at this site. The first was a bridge that was built in the 1890s. After the structure deteriorated, a second bridge was constructed in the 1960s. This also fell into disrepair. Local citizens pressed for a new bridge and started a fund raising program. The existing bridge opened in 2011. It doesn't carry vehicle traffic.
World Index Number: SD/41-23-01
National Register of Historic Places: Not listed

Wisconsin County Map

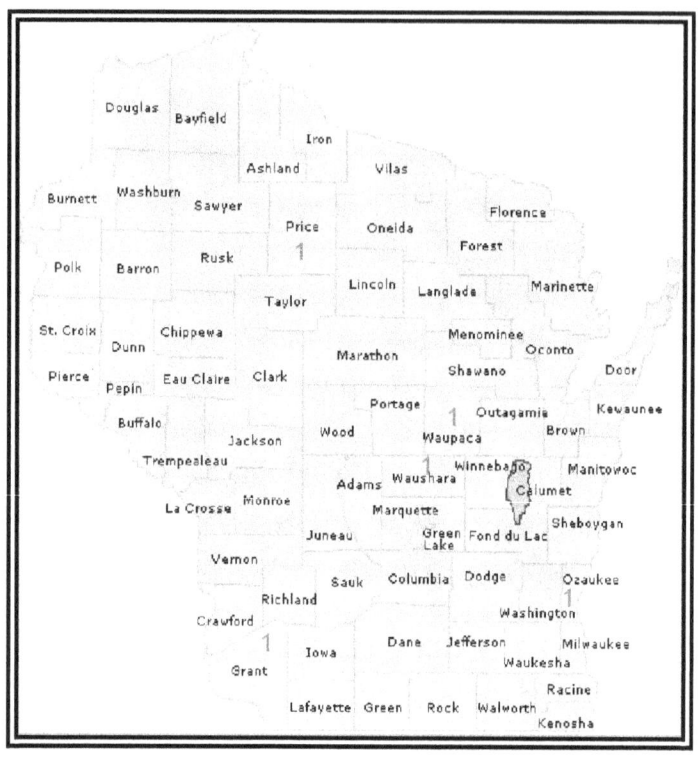

Stonefield Village Covered Bridge
County: Grant, Wisconsin
Township: Cassville

GPS Position: 42°43'47.0"N 91°01'03.0"W
Directions: From Cassville, head northwest on Co Hwy VV for 1.2 mi and turn left where the bridge is 0.1 mi
Crosses: Dewey Creek
Carries: Unnamed road
Builder: Grant County Highway Commission
Year Built: 1962
Truss Type: Howe
Dimensions: 1 Span, 51 feet
Notes: This bridge was built on a similar plan to the much older Cedarburg Covered Bridge, although very scaled down to suit the smaller length. It was built in pieces and given a specialized treatment for the wood in Minnesota before being shipped to the site for assembly.

World Index Number: WI/49-22-01
National Register of Historic Places: Not listed

Cedarburg Covered Bridge
County: Ozaukee, Wisconsin
Township: Cedarburg

GPS Position: 43°20'16.0"N 88°00'16.0"W
Directions: From Cedarburg, head north on Covered Bridge Rd from WI-60 for 0.9 mi to find the bridge
Crosses: Cedar Creek
Carries: Covered Bridge Rd
Builder: Michael Hickey
Year Built: 1876 (M1927) (R1927) (R2009)
Truss Type: Town
Dimensions: 1+ Span, 120 feet
Notes: This bridge is often described as the last covered bridge in Wisconsin. It would be more accurate to call it the last historical bridge as the others were built in the last part of the 20th century. It was bypassed in 1962 and moved 50 feet as well. In 1927 a center pier was added.

World Index Number: WI/49-46-01
National Register of Historic Places: March 14, 1973

Smith Rapids (Chequamegon) CB
County: Price, Wisconsin
Township: Chequamegon

GPS Position: 45°54'40.0"N 90°10'19.0"W
Directions: From Field, head east on WI-70 E toward for 12.4 mi and turn left onto Smith Rapids Rd. After 1.2 mi turn left to stay on Smith Rapids Rd and the bridge is 0.7 mi
Crosses: South Fork, Flambeau River
Carries: Smith Rapids Rd
Builder: Not known
Year Built: 1991
Truss Type: Town
Dimensions: 1 Span, 94 feet
Notes: This bridge is located in the Chequamegon-Nicolet National Forest, a popular destination for leisure activities such as canoeing and bird watching. There are also adjacent picnic tables, grilling facilities and toilets. There is an admission charge.
World Index Number: WI/49-51-01
National Register of Historic Places: Not listed

Red Mill Covered Bridge
County: Waupaca, Wisconsin
Township: Dayton

GPS Position: 44°19'06.0"N 89°06'30.0"W
Directions: From Waupaca, head SW on Lakeside Pkwy for 0.7 mi and continue on WI-22 S. After 0.7 mi, turn left at County Rd K. In 1.3 mi go left on Crystal Rd to find the bridge
Crosses: Crystal River
Carries: Crystal Rd
Builder: Not known
Year Built: 1970
Truss Type: Town
Dimensions: 1 Span, 40 feet
Notes: The bridge is located behind the 1855 Red Mill, proceed through the walkway in the mill. There is also a Gift Shop and Wedding Chapel at the site. This is the shortest Wisconsin Covered Bridge.

World Index Number: WI/49-69-01
National Register of Historic Places: Not listed

Springwater Volunteer Covered Bridge
County: Waushara, Wisconsin
Township: Springwater

GPS Position: 44°10'46.0"N 89°08'01.0"W
Directions: From Saxeville, head west on Portage St for 1.0 mi and turn right onto to find the bridge
Crosses: Pine River
Carries: Covered Bridge Rd
Builder: Local volunteers
Year Built: 1997
Truss Type: Town
Dimensions: 1 Span, 44 feet
Notes: In 1989, an old concrete bridge needed replacement and the authorities decided on a new concrete structure although many locals called for a covered bridge. The volunteers fund raised to raise a separate bridge they would build themselves. They built a smaller replica of the Cedarburg Covered Bridge which opened in 1997.
World Index Number: WI/49-70-01
National Register of Historic Places: Not listed

Wisconsin Tour

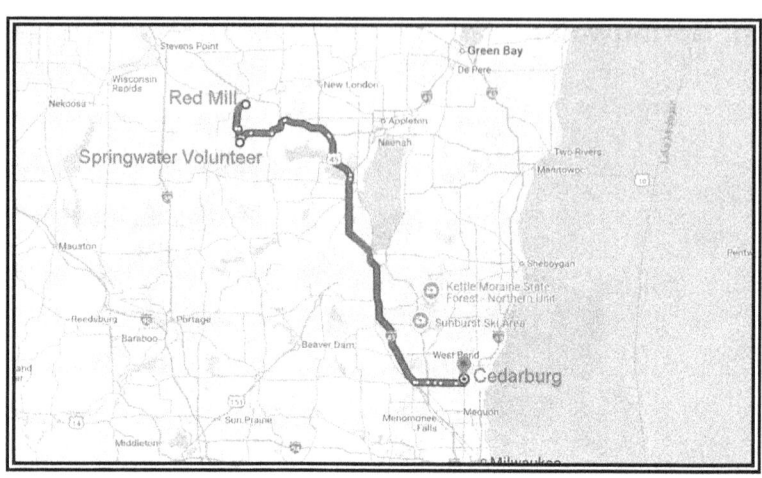

3 bridges, 2 hours driving

Red Mill 44°19'06.0"N 89°06'30.0"W
Springwater Volunteer 44°10'46.0"N 89°08'01.0"W
Cedarburg 43°20'16.0"N 88°00'16.0"W

Glossary

Abutment: The abutments are the bridge supports on each side bank. Usually they were originally constructed of stone but they have often been replaced or supplemented with concrete through the years.

Arch: A curved timber or timber set which is shaped in a curve and functions as a support of the bridge.

Bed timbers: Timbers between the abutment and the truss or bottom chord.

Brace or bracing: A diagonal timber or timber set used to support the trusses.

Bridge Deck: The roadway through the bridge.

Buttress: Wood or metal members on the exterior sides which connect the floor beams and the top of the truss. Used to keep the bridge structure from twisting under wind, water and snow loads.

Camber: A planned curve in the structure to compensate for the weight of the structure.

Chord: The horizontal members extending the length of the truss meant to carry the load to the abutments.

Dead load: The load of the weight of the bridge itself.

Deck: The pathway through the bridge used by pedestrians or vehicles.

Pier: Stone/concrete supports built in the stream bed to support the bridge

Portal: The bridge's entrances.

Post: The truss's vertical members.

Span: The bridge length measured between the abutments.

Treenails or trunnels: Pins or dowels turned from hardwood, driven into holes drilled into the members of the truss to hold them together. Also used in mortised joints.

Truss: The framework which carries the load of the bridge and distributes it to the abutments.

Truss Types

A Truss is a system of ties and struts which are connected to act like a single beam to distribute and carry a load. In covered bridges, these Trusses carry the load to stone abutments at each side and perhaps piers in between.

Brown

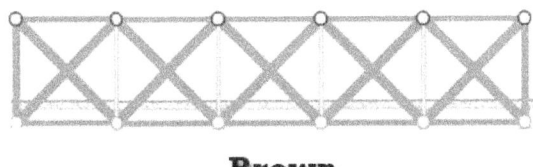

Brown

Josiah Brown Jr., of Buffalo, New York, patented this system in 1857. It consists of diagonal cross compression members connected to horizontal top and bottom stringers and is known for economic use of materials. It was only used in Michigan where there are a couple of surviving members.

Burr Arch

Burr Arch

Invented in 1804 by Theodore Burr, the Burr Arch is one of the most commonly found structures in Covered Bridge design. It is often used in combination with multiple kingposts. The ends of the arch are buried in the abutments

Childs

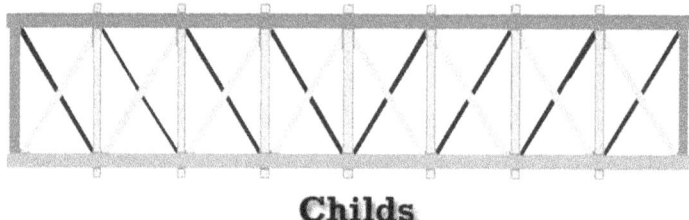

The Childs Truss System is essentially a multiple kingpost with half of the diagonal timbers replaced with iron bars.

Howe

The Howe Truss was patented in 1840 by William Howe. It involves the use of vertical metal rods between the joints of wooden diagonals.

Kingpost

Kingpost is the simplest form of Truss with two diagonal members on a bottom chord, often with a vertical post connecting to the diagonals. The multiple Kingpost involves a series of Kingposts symmetrical from the bridges center. This allows for a much longer span.

Long

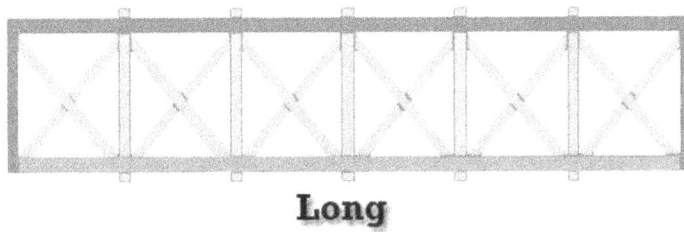

The Long Truss was patented by Stephen Long in 1830. It is a series of X shaped diagonals connected to vertical posts

Paddleford

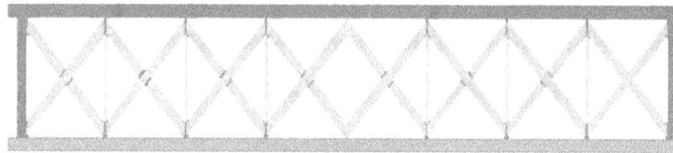
Paddleford

Peter Paddleford worked with the Long Truss system and eventually adapted it with a system of interlocking braces. he was never able to patent the system due to challenges from the owners of the Long Truss patent. However there are a number of New Hampshire and Vermont bridges which use the Paddleford system

Partridge

Partridge

Reuben L. Partridge received a patent for a design similar to the Smith system but adding terminal braces at the end and a central vertical member.

Pratt

Pratt

The Pratt truss was patented in 1844 by Caleb Pratt and his son Thomas Willis Pratt. The design uses vertical members for compression and horizontal members to respond to tension.

Queenpost

Queenpost Truss

The Queenpost has the peak of the kingpost type replaced with a horizontal top chord which allows for a longer span.

Smith

Robert W. Smith received patents in 1867 and 1869 for variations of his system.

Town

The Town or lattice system was patented by Ithiel Town in 1820. It involved a system of overlapping diagonals in a lattice pattern connected at the intersection by Tree nails or trunnels, wooden pegs or dowels. It had the advantages in that it could be constructed by unskilled labor and local materials could be used.

Warren

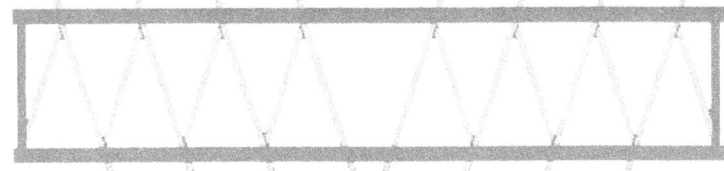

Warren

Patented in 1848 by two Englishmen, one of whom was named James Warren, it consists of parallel upper and lower chords with diagonal connecting members forming a series of equilateral triangles.

Recently Lost
The following bridges have been lost since 2000

Iowa
Delta Covered Bridge, IA/15-54-01x, Lost to arson 03 Sep 2003

Cedar Covered Bridge, IA/15-61-03#2x, Lost to arson 15 Apr 2017

References

National Society for the Preservation of Covered Bridges
http://www.coveredbridgesociety.org

New York State Covered Bridge Society
http://www.nycoveredbridges.org

Vermont Covered Bridge Society
http://www.vermontbridges.com/

Covered Bridge Society of Oregon
http://www.covered-bridges.org/

The Theodore Burr Covered Bridge Society of Pennsylvania
http://www.tbcbspa.com/

Indiana Covered Bridge Society
http://www.indianacrossings.org/

Ohio Historic Bridge Association
http://oldohiobridges.com/ohba/index.htm

Harold Stiver Image Gallery
https://haroldstiver.smugmug.com/Galleries/Themes/Covered-Bridges

Photo Credits:

Illinois
Jerrye and Roy Klotz MD, Captain Swift Covered Bridge
Nyttend, Thompson Mill Covered Bridge
Wayne Wilkinson, Red Covered Covered Bridge
All other Images by the author

Iowa
Jerrye and Roy Klotz MD, Hammond Covered Bridge
All other images by the author

Michigan
All images by the author

Minnesota
All images by the author

South Dakota
All images by the author

Wisconsin
Doug Kerr, Smith Rapids Covered Bridge
Heath Thiel, Stonefield Village Covered Bridge
All other Images by the author

The Photographer's and Explorer's Series

Unless noted, there are Print and eBook editions available for the following.

Birding Guide to Orkney
Guide to Photographing Birds

Maine Lighthouses
Ontario Lighthouses

Ontario's Old Mills

Ontario Waterfalls

Alabama Covered Bridges (eBook)
California Covered Bridges (eBook)
Canada's Covered Bridges
Connecticut Covered Bridges (eBook)
Georgia Covered Bridges (eBook)
Illinois Covered Bridges
Indiana Covered Bridges
Iowa Covered Bridges
Maine Covered Bridges (eBook)
Massachusetts Covered Bridges (eBook)
Michigan Covered Bridges (eBook)
Minnesota Covered Bridges
New Brunswick Covered Bridges
New England Covered Bridges
Covered Bridges of the Mid-Atlantic
Quebec Covered Bridges
Covered Bridges of the South
Missouri Covered Bridges
New Hampshire Covered Bridges

New York Covered Bridges
Ohio's Covered Bridges
Oregon Covered Bridges
The Covered Bridges of Kentucky (eBook)
The Covered Bridges of Kentucky and Tennessee
South Dakota Covered Bridge
Covered Bridges of the North
The Covered Bridges of Tennessee (eBook)
Vermont's Covered Bridges
The Covered Bridges of Virginia (eBook)
The Covered Bridges of Virginia and West Virginia
Washington Covered Bridges (eBook)
The Covered Bridges of West Virginia (eBook)
West Coast Covered Bridges
Wisconsin Covered Bridge

Indexes

Illinois Index
Allaman	19
Captain Swift	17
Eames	19
Glenarm	23
Hedley	23
Henderson County	19
Jackson	18
Little Mary's River	22
Red	16
Rockford Bolt Co.	15
Stickleback	20
Sugar Creek	23
Thompson Mill	24
Wolf	21
Young	15

Iowa Index
Cedar	33
Cutler	28
Donahoe	28
Hammond	34
Hogback	29
Holliwell	30
Imes	31
King	31
Knoxville	36
Mills	31
Munger	31
Oak Grove	32
Owens	37
Roseman	32
Wilcox Game Preserve	35

Michigan Index
Ackley	46
Ada	42
Bradfield	42
Fallasburg	43
Holtz Brucke	44
Langley	45
White's	41
Zehnder	44

Minnesota Index
Zumbrota	49

South Dakota Index
Edgemount City Park	51

Wisconsin Index
Cedarburg	54
Chequamegon	55
Red Mill	56
Smith Rapids	55
Springwater Volunteer	57
Stonefield Village	53

www.ingramcontent.com/pod-product-compliance
Lightning Source LLC
Chambersburg PA
CBHW031419040426
42444CB00005B/641